FIRE-FIGHTING VEHICLES IN PRESERVATION

MALCOLM BATTEN

AMBERLEY

First published 2025

Amberley Publishing
The Hill, Stroud
Gloucestershire, GL5 4EP

www.amberley-books.com

Copyright © Malcolm Batten, 2025

The right of Malcolm Batten to be identified as the Author of this work has been asserted in accordance with the Copyrights, Designs and Patents Act 1988.

ISBN: 978 1 3981 2559 9 (print)
ISBN: 978 1 3981 2560 5 (ebook)

All rights reserved. No part of this book may be reprinted or reproduced or utilised in any form or by any electronic, mechanical or other means, now known or hereafter invented, including photocopying and recording, or in any information storage or retrieval system, without the permission in writing from the Publishers.

British Library Cataloguing in Publication Data.
A catalogue record for this book is available from the British Library.

Typeset by Simon and Sons ITES Services Pvt. Ltd., Chennai, India.
Printed in Great Britain.

Appointed GPSR EU Representative: Easy Access System Europe Oü, 16879218

Address: Mustamäe tee 50, 10621, Tallinn, Estonia
Contact Details: gpsr.requests@easproject.com, +358 40 500 3575

Introduction

The danger of fire has long been appreciated. It was tragically demonstrated by the Great Fire of London in 1666, which destroyed much of the medieval city including the old St Paul's Cathedral. At the time parish churches were required to stock buckets, ladders, axes and firehooks for residents to fight fires and pull down damaged buildings. Although water from the Thames was available to fight the blaze, there were no effective hoses and the use of bucket gangs to fight it was minimal as the inhabitants tried initially to move their possessions to safer areas and later to flee the conflagration. In the end, it was a drop in the wind and the belated use of explosives to create firebreaks that ended the fire, which it is estimated destroyed over 13,000 houses, plus numerous other buildings.

Despite this, however, public fire services were not instigated until the nineteenth century. Before then, buildings could be insured with fire insurance companies, who would retain pumps and send people to help extinguish fires but only in properties insured with them. The saving of lives was not the main concern of these companies.

The world's first municipal fire brigade was set up in Edinburgh in 1824, led by James Braidwood (1800–61). He set up systems of operation that became the basis for other fire brigades. In 1830 he published the first book on fire engineering, *On the Construction of Fire Engines and Apparatus*. Braidwood became Superintendent of the London Fire Engine Establishment in 1833, which brought together ten of the insurance company brigades.

In London, the inadequacies of not having a public fire service were highlighted by two key events. In October 1834 a fire almost totally destroyed the old Palace of Westminster. Then in 1861 a fire broke out at Cotton's Wharf in Tooley Street, which took two weeks to extinguish and caused millions of pounds worth of damage. James Braidwood was killed in this fire when a wall collapsed on him. The insurance companies asked Parliament to relieve them of their responsibilities. As a result, the Metropolitan Fire Brigade was created in 1866 under the responsibility of the Metropolitan Board of Works and with Captain Sir Eyre Massey Shaw as its first commander. This then became the London Fire Brigade in 1904.

At the time of the MFB's creation the only equipment available was hand-operated pumps. However, steam power was already established on the railways and road traction engines were being developed. In the 1860s horse-drawn steam-powered fire pumps began to be produced and these became more established from the 1870s. Two London-based companies came to dominate this market: Merryweather & Sons Ltd and Shand-Mason & Co. Shand-Mason were in production until taken over by their rivals in 1928. Both companies did go on to build a few self-propelled steam fire engines but none have survived in Great Britain.

With the development of the internal combustion engine towards the end of the nineteenth century, it was not long before the technology was applied to fire appliances. By the time of the outbreak of the First World War, petrol-powered buses, lorries and fire engines were rapidly taking over from horses and steam power. This would be the first war to make use of such vehicles and the War Office conducted trials beforehand to establish the best-performing vehicles.

Vehicle design progressed rapidly in the 1920s and 1930s with the introduction of pneumatic tyres and enclosed cabs, although most turntable ladder escapes continued to have open cabs. A common body design from the 1910s to 1930s was the Braidwood style whereby the hose and equipment were housed in a central box area while the crew sat or stood on the side facing outwards and held on to the ladder for support – a design harping back to the horse-drawn era and increasingly unsafe as vehicle speeds increased.

A system of local government had been established by Acts of 1888 and 1894 with County Councils, County Borough Councils, and below these Urban and Rural District Councils and Parish Councils. Fire brigades were set up by each of these, such that by 1938 there were some 1,600 separate local fire brigades.

In 1938, with war becoming a likely possibility, a parallel Auxiliary Fire Service of mainly volunteers was set up in each fire authority along with air-raid precautions.

When the Second World War did break out, the danger from aerial bombing during the Battle of Britain put enormous pressure on fire services. In August 1941 the National Fire Service (NFS) was created by amalgamating the Auxiliary Fire Service with the local authority fire brigades. The NFS comprised both full-time and part-time members, both men and women. At its peak there were some 370,000 personnel including 80,000 women, although these were mainly in administrative roles. As well as fighting fires, members had to clear up the aftermath of German bombing raids and coastal shelling. Large numbers of vehicles were acquired by the NFS, painted in a distinctive grey livery to make them less conspicuous. The NFS remained in charge until 1948 when fire services reverted to local authority control as a result of the Fire Services Act 1947. However, it was now only the counties and county boroughs that had fire brigades, so the number was substantially reduced. When the NFS was disbanded, many of their vehicles were transferred to the local fire brigades and repainted red.

In 1948 the Auxiliary Fire Service was reformed as a national fire reserve. With the Cold War and fears of a nuclear attack, the AFS took on responsibilities for Civil Defence. A large fleet of Bedford RL 'Green Goddess' fire engines was built for the Auxiliary Fire Service. They would be used in conjunction with other vehicles such as hose layers, bridge units, command vehicles, etc., to make up Emergency Mobile Columns which would enter a bombed area following a nuclear attack. The 'Green Goddesses' would bring fresh water and fight fires. The AFS was disbanded in 1968 and the vehicles were mothballed in government stores. They were brought out of reserve during the fire fighters strikes of 1977–78 and 2002–03, thus seeing active use for the first time.

Local government reforms have seen further mergers of fire brigades as in London from 1965 when the London Fire Brigade absorbed former local authority fleets, as well as the Middlesex County Council. Boundary changes have also seen some fire stations and their vehicles moving to different brigades. In 1973 there were about 150 fire brigades in the United Kingdom.

Fire engines were not only bought by fire brigades. Many major manufacturing companies had a works fire engine to deal with any incidents on their premises. A few were also bought by the owners of large estates. Another specialised form of fire fighting was at airfields where vehicles were deployed to deal with any crashes or fires on aircraft.

While many of the British manufacturers of commercial vehicles also made fire-fighting vehicles, certain names come to the forefront as specialists in this field. Foremost of these must be Dennis Bros (founded 1895), a company still making such vehicles until 2007 and still in business making buses as Alexander Dennis. AEC, Leyland, Bedford, Commer and Karrier were also major players in this market and many vehicles from each of these companies have survived. Until around the 1990s, almost all British fire appliances would have been British made. Specialist body builders also came to be associated with this market, often fitting out the vehicles to the client's specification. Merryweather & Sons continued manufacture, moving on from steam to motorised fire engines built on various chassis makes, plus ladders and pumps. By the start of the twenty-first century they were no longer making fire engines but making and servicing fire extinguishers and other fire-fighting equipment. The company name was officially discontinued in November 2023 when they became part of Morgan Fire Protection Ltd.

Fire-fighting vehicles would be maintained in tip-top condition because they needed to be available whenever required. Consequently, when preservation of commercial vehicles became established they were a popular choice with preservationists. Indeed, many came to be preserved by firefighters themselves. Some would be retained as heritage vehicles by the fire brigades and brought out for civic parades and events raising money for fire charities. Many others have been saved and placed in local museum collections. There is a Fire Service Preservation Group, which was founded in 1968 by former members of the Auxiliary Fire Service and is now the UK's largest group of preservationists and re-enactors.

Preserved fire-fighting vehicles can frequently be seen at vehicle rallies, traction engine rallies and road runs. Events like the road runs of the Historic Commercial Vehicle Society, including the London to Brighton Run, held most years since 1962 always feature a selection of such vehicles. This event often attracts entries from mainland Europe, contrasting with our home-produced designs. Furthermore, many such vehicles have been imported from the United States by preservationists and these can also be seen participating at such events.

In this book I have referred to 'fire-fighting vehicles' rather than 'fire engines'. This is to recognise that a wide range of vehicles were operated by fire services, not all of which were to put out fires. There would be command vehicles, hose layers, turntable escapes, recovery trucks, etc., and examples of all these types have passed into preservation. This book features a variety of the vehicles preserved from the early horse-drawn hand pumps to the 1990s. While British-built vehicles predominate, there are also examples of the European and American vehicles that have also attended events in this country. A particular feature of American practice, probably the result of their earlier development of high-rise buildings, has been the use of articulated ladder escapes, allowing a longer ladder than practical on a rigid vehicle.

All photographs are by the author. Please note that the term 'present owner' used in the captions refers to the owner at the time the vehicle was photographed – this may have changed since then.

Hand Pumps

Seen outside a local museum in the village of Bloxham, Oxfordshire, in 2015, this horse-drawn hand pump is typical of the type of equipment that would have been available in the early part of the nineteenth century. The plates on the frame state (in Roman numerals) that it was built by Newsham & Ragg of London in 1749 and repaired in 1892. It was bought by subscription for the parish of Bloxham.

Seen at the Expo Steam rally held at Peterborough Showground in August 1982 is this pony-drawn hand fire pump. The crew would raise and lower the wooden bars on either side of the vehicle to pump water through the hose. This was hard work and they would not be able to sustain for very long. A steam fire pump can be seen behind this, and various motor fire engines are parked up alongside.

The company that became Shand-Mason & Co. was founded in 1760 by Samuel Phillips, the eventual name being adopted in the 1850s. Initially hand-operated pumps were made, such as this example preserved on the Epping Ongar Railway. Their first steam fire pump for the Metropolitan Fire Brigade in London was supplied in 1860.

Horse-drawn Steam Pumps

The oldest working Shand-Mason fire engine in the world is *St George*, built in 1876. This was built as a single-cylinder works fire engine for Sedgwicks Watford Brewery, where it served until 1913 when it returned to Shand-Mason for refurbishment and was sold on to a Norfolk country estate. Restoration started in 1979 and a new boiler was fitted in 1994. This regularly attends events around Hertfordshire and Bedfordshire and is seen here at the Enfield Pageant of Motoring in May 1987.

Dating from 1890, this Shand-Mason fire engine was Metropolitan Fire Brigade No. P3. Now preserved by the London Museum of Water & Steam, Kew, it was lettered for the Metropolitan Water Board when attending the Fawley Hill Vintage Festival in 2016.

This Shand-Mason was built in 1894 for the Great North of Scotland Railway. When seen here in 1988 it was an exhibit at the former Glasgow Transport Museum at Kelvin Hall, now replaced by the new Riverside Museum. The fire engine is now on loan to the Grampian Transport Museum.

St Giles is a two-cylinder Shand-Mason dating from 1908. This was photographed at Battersea Park, London, in 2000 when it was attending the London Harness Horse Parade, which was held each year on Easter Monday. This event, although still called the London Harness Horse Parade, no longer takes place in London but at the South of England Showground at Ardingly, West Sussex. This type of engine could raise steam from cold water in less than ten minutes while travelling to a fire.

This 1909 Shand-Mason originally served on the Duke of Bedford's estate. During the Second World War it was located by the NFS at Thorney, Cambridgeshire. In 1971 it was put on display at the Bedfordshire Fire Brigade HQ at Kempston. Since then, it has been restored by apprentices of W. H. Allen Engineering. This is now kept at Biggleswade Fire Station and makes regular rally appearances such as here at St Albans in 2009.

This Shand-Mason dates from 1912 and was supplied to Ely Fire Brigade. It looks somewhat different because it was later mounted on road wheels with pneumatic tyres and would have been towed by a lorry. After being stored for thirty years this was restored in 2011 and is now kept at the Prickwillow Engine Museum. It was attending the Weeting Steam Engine Rally in 2018.

Fire-fighting Vehicles in Preservation

The company that later became Merryweather & Sons dates back to 1690 when founded by Nathaniel Hadley. Second oldest of the Merryweather steam fire engines preserved in Britain is this *c.* 1880 engine from Gateshead. Part of the National Railway Museum collection, it was on display at York in 2000 but has since been moved to the subsidiary collection at Shildon, County Durham.

Looking perhaps older than its date of *c.* 1890, this Merryweather engine, No. 1150, served Tehidy House, a large country estate near Camborne, Cornwall.

Merryweather engine No. 3254 was supplied to Prudhoe Urban District Council in Northumberland. This is preserved at the Newcastle Discovery Museum, but in July 1989 it was attending an event at Duxford Airfield, Cambridgeshire.

Merryweather continued making steam fire pump trailers long after they ceased making horse-drawn engines. This typical example was seen at Netley Marsh near Southampton in 2000.

Making an interesting contrast to the British-built engines, this 1908 Bikkers engine was built in Rotterdam for the Leiden Fire Brigade. It was brought to the Weeting Steam Engine Rally in 1998 by the Historic Fire Engine Society of the Netherlands and believed to be its first trip to the UK. Designed to be hauled by a single horse, it has a four-cylinder engine and an oil-fired boiler. It was restored between 1985 and 1991 and the boiler was rebuilt in 1996–97.

British Motor Vehicles to 1919

The first motorised fire engine in London was supplied by Merryweather & Sons to Finchley District Council in 1904, at a time when horse-drawn steam pumps were the norm. This is now part of the collection of the Science Museum, London. It was on display in the transport gallery during 1982 when this photo was taken but is now part of the reserve collection and not on public display.

One of the oldest working motorised fire engines, CR1500 was built in 1912 by John Morris & Sons of Manchester on a six-cylinder Belsize chassis. It served with Southampton Fire Brigade until 1926 when it was part-exchanged with Dennis for a new appliance. It was then fitted with pneumatic tyres and sold to Billings of Guildford, who kept it until the late 1950s. It was rescued in 1961, took part in the first HCVC London–Brighton Run in 1962 and was back for the fiftieth Run in 2011. One of only two known surviving Belsize fire engines, it is owned by the Enfield & District Veteran Vehicle Society. Seen here at the Enfield Pageant of Motoring in 1987.

Dennis Bros built their first fire engine in 1908. This Dennis motorised portable trailer pump dates from 1913, and is one of two supplied to the Great Eastern Railway for use at their Stratford railway workshops. Previously part of the Science Museum reserve collection at Wroughton, it is now cared for at the Bressingham Steam Museum. This was on display at Brooklands Museum, Weybridge, during their Summer Festival in June 2025. Apparently only four of this design were built, the other two being exported to the King of Siam (Thailand). Note the unusual design of wheels. This is the fourth oldest Dennis fire appliance listed as preserved by the Dennis Society and the oldest trailer pump.

ED 810 is a 1914 Dennis N supplied new to Greenall Whitney brewery in Warrington where it remained until 1950. It was restored by Dennis in the late 1950s and then took part in the first London–Brighton Run. It repeated this feat several times in the 1960s but by the 1980s had retired to a motoring museum in the Lake District. However, it returned to Brighton in 2011 for the fiftieth anniversary Run.

DU 179, a 1914 Dennis N, was the first motorised fire engine to be bought by the City of Coventry. It worked for twenty-two years, then was sold to GEC's Stoke works for another twenty-two years. It was then reacquired by the makers Dennis Bros for £35 in 1958 for preservation. This is original except for the pneumatic tyres – a conversion made by Dennis in 1936. It took part in the inaugural London–Brighton Run in 1962 and has been back many times since, as well as attending other events such as here at Rushmoor Arena in 1995.

Probably the best-known preserved fire engine, LP 8389 *Jezebel* is a 1916 Dennis N fire engine which worked for the London Fire Brigade at Vauxhall Fire Station from 1916 until 1932. It was then sold to Joseph Crossfield & Sons Ltd of Warrington before being donated to the Royal College of Science Motor Club at Imperial College in 1955, who have maintained it ever since. It was entered at the first London–Brighton Run in 1962 and has been a regular participant ever since. It is seen here arriving at the finish in 2006.

LR 9674 is a 1918 Leyland fire engine new to the London Fire Brigade. When photographed at the Peterborough Expo rally in 1981 it was lettered for subsequent owners John Haig & Co. Ltd, who used it at their Markinch distillery. Similar LR 9675 is also in preservation.

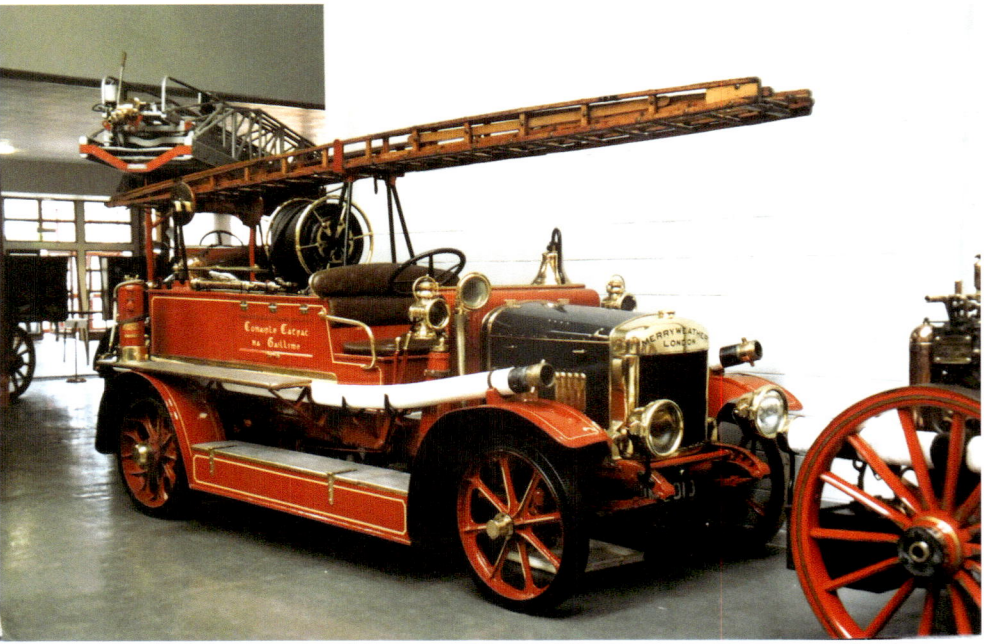

IM 3010 is a Merryweather-badged fire engine registered in Galway, Ireland. This was housed in the Glasgow Transport Museum at Kelvin Hall (since relocated) in 1988.

British Vehicles of the 1920s

FA1075 is a 1921 Dennis N that was new to the Bass Ratcliff & Gretton brewery at Burton-on-Trent. It is fitted with a 10-litre White & Poppe four-cylinder engine and a Gwynne three-stage pump capable of pumping 900 gallons per minute (gpm). The Merryweather ladder extends 50 feet. The works fire engine could be called out to assist the local fire brigade up to 10 miles away and the works fire crew were paid an extra 1*s* for each call out. The Dennis served for forty-five years. This was first entered at Brighton in 1996 and then frequently until 2010. This view is from 2003.

Seen at the Peterborough Expo Steam Rally in 1984, XU 9993 is a 1922 Gwynne Eight pump. It was built as a prototype and demonstrator before being sold in 1925 to Mountnessing village in Essex. When the village fire service was absorbed into the National Fire Service, XU 9993 was sold to the Marconi Wireless & Telegraph Company (now GEC Marconi) at Chelmsford where it remained until 1954. It was then displayed at the Essex Fire Brigade's Brentwood HQ until 1962. In 1968 it was reacquired by GEC Marconi and restored.

TC 6851 is a 1923 model T Ford fire appliance that was supplied to Edward, Earl of Derby. This was taken at the Gloucestershire Vintage and Country Fayre in 2017.

ML 255 is a 1925 Austin type 20/4 pump/escape. It was originally built as a limousine and used as a taxi. In 1936 it was converted to a fire engine for use at Brighton Mental Hospital and later at the St Francis Hospital, Haywards Heath. It was used with a Dennis trailer pump until 1939, then laid up until rescued for preservation in 1963. Restoration was undertaken in 1999–2001 and it was first entered on the London–Brighton Run in 2001.

Built in 1929, ARB 165 is a Merryweather fire engine with Braidwood body based on an Albion chassis with a 65-bhp engine. It has a Merryweather piston pump with a vertical air chamber to equalise the pressure from the different pistons. This served at the Staveley Coal & Iron Company plant near Chesterfield until 1971 when it was sold into preservation. It was an exhibit at the 1985 Peterborough Expo rally.

A regular entrant at Brighton in the early 2000s, PN 4119 is a 1929 Dennis with Braidwood body bought by Hove Borough Council. It was requisitioned by the National Fire Service in 1941 and returned to service after the war. In 1952 it was sold to Baker Perkins, Peterborough, as their works fire engine. In 1995 it was repurchased by Hove Borough and is now kept in a purpose-built fire station at the Amberley Museum in West Sussex.

UD 2682 is a Morris first registered in 1929. Built as a demonstrator, it served as a works fire appliance for Morris Motors at their Cowley factory until replaced by a Morris Minor in 1952 (see p. 48). It was then sold to a member of staff, who removed the fire equipment to create a two-seater car. It was later rescued from a scrapyard and rebuilt to original form. Only five others of this design were built. Two were sold to the City of Oxford Fire Service in 1931, two to Worthing Town Council and the final one was exported to a Maharajah in India.

British Vehicles of the 1930s

We saw earlier a Dennis fire engine of 1921 that saw service in Burton-on-Trent (see p. 17). The progress in design through the 1920s can be compared in this view of a 1930 Dennis that also saw service in the same town with the local fire brigade. FA 4067 retains the open cab layout that would continue through the 1930s for ladder escapes but pneumatic tyres on disc rather than spoked wheels was now the norm. This has a Dennis 'low-loader' chassis, and a 1,000-gpm Dennis No. 3 pump with 75-gallon tank. The cost new was £1,485. Taken at Brighton, 1995.

Morris-Commercial KJ 14 was new to the Dartford Rural District Council in 1931 with bodywork by the local coachbuilding firm of Beadle. It was converted to a generator unit after the war. This was found derelict at New Romney in 1968 and rebuilt to original specification from contemporary photographs.

Fire-fighting Vehicles in Preservation 21

HY 1801 is a Leyland Lioness LTB1 pump/escape with Leyland bodywork that was built as a prototype for Bristol in 1931. The design was so successful that these Leylands became a staple for many other fire brigades. HY 1801 remained in use until 1963, then passed through various owners before full restoration from 1994 onwards.

This superbly presented Leyland FT1 pump/escape also dates from 1931 when it was purchased for £1,500 by the Borough of Wisbech Fire Brigade and named *Vivien* by the mayoress. It saw service until 1963, then passed straight into preservation. In *c.* 2004 the then owners formed the Vivien Fire Engine Trust as a charity that promotes fire safety and educates the public. This has visited Brighton on a number of occasions, as here in 2004.

Looking rather strange in green rather than the more normal red livery, JH 8235 is a 1934 Dennis Big 4 pump escape that was originally supplied to Letchworth Garden City Fire Brigade and then passed to Hertfordshire Fire Brigade where it worked until 1963. This is fitted with a Dennis No. 3 main pump and a 50-foot Merryweather wheeled escape ladder. In 1966 this appliance was driven from London to Paris by its then owner Paul Adorian to mark the 300th anniversary of the Great Fire of London. Taken at Brighton in 1990.

Dating from 1934, this Morris Commercial C type was lettered for the Romford Brewery Company when seen at the 1995 North Weald Rally. Registered at Burton-on-Trent, it was apparently rebuilt from a dray lorry to serve as a works fire engine. It must have been in preservation for a considerable time by then to judge from the number of rally plaques displayed.

AUR 551 is a 1935 Leyland Cub FK4 model pump/escape that served the Bishop's Stortford Fire Brigade until 1963 when it retired into preservation. Still active, this was it at the Bedfordshire Steam & Country Fayre in 2016.

BOF 389 is a Leyland Tigress new to the Birmingham Fire Brigade in 1935. It is fitted with a Metz 104-foot turntable ladder. The radiator badge is lettered 'BFB' for Birmingham Fire Brigade rather than displaying the maker's name. Taken at Ardingly Showground in 1984, this is now resident at the Wythall Bus Museum near Birmingham.

Also in green livery is AAP 344, a 1936 Dennis Light Six pump with Braidwood body. This worked for Crowborough, then East Sussex until 1961 and then for Lyons Tea. It was later offered as a prize by them and was won by students from Sussex University. It was derelict by 1982 when bought for preservation. The Crowborough Volunteer Firemen raised by door-to-door collection the £1,250 to buy the appliance which had served the town until 1956. Named *Frank Humphry* after the local businessman who initiated the building of the first fire station in the town in 1904.

Waiting to enter the ring at the 1987 Knowl Hill Rally is GV 4619. This 1936 Morris Commercial with Merryweather body was owned by the Greene King brewery at Bury St Edmunds. Retired in 1960, it was rescued in 1975 and restored over the next four years.

In 1936 Dennis built this Big 6 fire engine for Swansea Fire Brigade at a cost of £1,368. It must have been good value, as it remained in use until 1965. It was found in a field in Essex and bought for preservation in 1984.

BYV 321 is a 1936 Dennis Lancet chassis badged as a Morris/Magirus. Built for the London Fire Brigade, it has John Morris bodywork with a Magirus ladder. This served at Manchester Square station until 1963 and was withdrawn in 1965. Seen at Redhill in 2011. Similar BYV 322 also survives. It was at Kensington until 1965 and was withdrawn in 1967, being then sold to the Irish Railways and later preserved in Ireland. It returned to the UK in 2022 and was undergoing restoration in 2025. BYV 323 was destroyed in an air raid during the Blitz in 1940.

This Dennis Ace has the 'New World' body design, which was an intermediate style between the earlier open designs and the later enclosed vehicles. The crew sit inside the rear facing inwards. FPC 448 of 1936 was the Dennis Works fire engine and was still operational until *c.* 1996. It was also regularly rallied as seen here at Southsea in 1990. This has been retained as a heritage vehicle by Alexander Dennis Ltd as successors to the makers. It is fitted with a Dennis No. 2 pump delivering 500 gallons per minute.

Dating from a year later, EBH 823 is a 1937 Dennis Ace with Dennis body new to Beaconsfield UDC. It was taken over by the NFS in wartime and later transferred to Buckinghamshire County Council in 1948. In 1961 it was sold to Wiggins Teape for £84 and served at their paper mill until 1996. It was on display at the Dennis Works Open Day at Guildford in May 2019.

DHA 555 is a 1937 Leyland Cub FK6 fire engine supplied to Cape Hill Brewery (Mitchell & Butlers) Fire Brigade. It saw wartime service in the Birmingham area. It has been in preservation with the same owners since in the 1970s. Bought as parts, it was finally restored in 2012.

FW 9658 is a 1937 Leyland Lynx with Braidwood body supplied to Skegness Urban District Council. It served with the AFS and NFS and was later absorbed into the Lindsey County Fire Service. It was purchased in 1990 and restored to original condition for this appearance at Brighton in 1993.

DGJ 309 is a 1937 Leyland TLM open-cab turntable fire escape fitted with a Metz four section 101-foot ladder and a 500-gallon-per-minute Rees fire pump. It spent its entire working life based at Soho Fire Station, London, until withdrawn in 1964. It was then stored by a dealer until purchased for restoration in 1981. It has attended many events, including the 1983 Royal Tournament, and appeared in several films. Note the two bells (no sirens in those days) and the white markings on the mudguards to aid visibility in the blackout during the Second World War.

CDD 121 is a 1937 Fordson with Drysdale pump that was bought as a works appliance for R. A. Lister & Co., Dursley, Gloucestershire, where it stayed until the 1980s. It was then sold to Birnbeck Island, Weston-super-Mare, as it was small enough to cross the pier to the island. Now preserved and restored, it was seen at the Gloucestershire Vintage & Country Extravaganza in 2018. Its first rally was the 2017 Brighton Run.

EBM 177, a 1938 Bedford MSC, was a works fire engine for its makers, Vauxhall Motors. It started out as a dropside lorry in the factory. The workshop added a crew cab and a 50-foot escape ladder. Taken at a Bedford Society event at Cambridge in 2003, this now resides at the Anglesey Transport Museum.

HPJ 382 is a 1938 Dennis 'Big Four' appliance that was new to the Vickers Armstrong aircraft factory at Brooklands. During the war it was sent to Portsmouth but returned and remained until 1971. It was then restored and maintained by firemen at Basingstoke Fire Station for thirty years. It still remains in Basingstoke but is now displayed at the Milestones Museum when not making rally appearances.

FP 3564 is a 1938 Dennis Light Four registered in the County of Rutland. It was new to the Oakham & Uppingham Joint Fire Brigade. This has a Merryweather ladder and a Dennis No. 2 pump. It has been in preservation since the early 1960s.

This open-cab Bedford was supplied to Wareham Fire Brigade in Dorset during 1939. It has survived and was photographed at Basingstoke in 2001.

Also dating from 1939, this Bedford MLZ fire engine has an enclosed cab. This was supplied to the Boston Rural District Council and later passed to the Holland County Fire Service in Lincolnshire. The bodywork was allegedly built by the local undertaker! It towed a Scammell trailer pump originally and had a 200-gallon tank behind the cab. Seen here at the 1988 Great Dorset Steam Fair.

This is a *c.* 1939 Commer Q3 with Merryweather body and equipment. This was new to Short Bros at Rochester. In 1942 it passed to Vickers Armstrong at Winchester and later at South Marston where it was used until 1963 and then stored. In 1973 it was donated to Portsmouth City Museum, but in 1992 it was donated on to the Brooklands Museum Trust.

BPM 212 is a 1939 Dennis 'New World' Light Four from East Sussex where it was stationed at Hurstpierpoint until the 1960s except for a stint in use in London during the war. After withdrawal it passed to CIBA laboratories for a further ten years until purchased for preservation in 1984. Similar BPM 213, which was based at Turners Hill, is also preserved.

BNR 421 is a 1939 Leyland that sports the unusual maroon livery adopted by the Leicestershire & Rutland Fire Service. This was at the Peterborough Expo Rally in 1984.

FLJ 356 is a 1939 Leyland Cub supplied to the Bournemouth Fire Brigade. This was at Netley Marsh near Southampton in 2000.

GKO 224 is a 1939 Leyland type FT4A pump escape that was new to Dartford Borough Fire Brigade. In 1948 it passed to the newly formed Kent Fire Brigade but remained at Dartford until 1955, then becoming a reserve machine for a year. It continued in use as a training vehicle until 1971. It was then restored in the brigade workshops as a museum vehicle maintained by Kent firemen. It was seen at a rally in its home town of Dartford in 2009.

HJO 834 is a 1939 Morris Commercial fire engine with Braidwood-style bodywork possibly by Merryweather. It was ordered for the royal estate at Windsor but with the onset of war it was diverted to become a works fire engine at the Morris works at Cowley near Oxford. It was sold off for preservation in 1969. The present owner acquired it in 1996. Seen at the Woodcote Rally in 2010.

Before the outbreak of war the Home Office ordered hundreds of vehicles that became allocated to the National Fire Service. FYH 104 is a 1939 Bedford WLG Heavy Unit. This was stationed at Woolston Fire Station in Southampton. It was found on a farm in 1984 and completely restored as seen at Brighton in 1996.

British Vehicles of the 1940s and Second World War

EBJ 852 is a Dennis Light Four pump appliance with 'New World'-style body dating from 1941. It was one of a pair bought by Gipping Rural District Council, later part of the Suffolk & Ipswich Fire Service. It served at Debenham, then Lowestoft. It was later sold to Cranfield's as a works fire engine at Ipswich Docks, then sold for preservation in 1978. This was at the Weeting Steam Rally in 1993.

This is known as a Ford model 7V Wartime Heavy Unit and dates from 1941. They were built to Home Office specifications for wartime use, many later passing into the fleets of local fire brigades. The history of this particular example is unknown. It has a Ford V8 engine and is fitted with a Tangye pump rated at 700 gallons per minute. This was seen at Basingstoke in 2011, now restored to NFS wartime grey livery with masked headlights for blackout conditions.

This *c.* 1941 Austin K4 was seen participating in the 2010 City of London Lord Mayor's Show.

Many thousands of these Austin K2 emergency fire tenders were built and supplied to the NFS. They operated with a trailer pump as seen here. GLC 793 dates from 1942. After serving in London during the war, like many others it was sold on and saw later use with Cornwall County Fire Brigade until 1974. Since preservation this has been rallied in both NFS grey and, as seen here, in London Fire Brigade red. Seen at Billericay, Essex, in 1998.

Another example of a 1942 Austin K2 fire tender. GLT 92 is preserved in NFS colours and served at Ruthin, North Wales, during the war. It was later a works fire engine for Stothart & Pitt. This was paired with a 1938 Coventry Climax trailer pump.

This Austin K2 was also new to the NFS and was later sold to the States of Guernsey Fire Brigade where it worked with a trailer pump. Now repatriated to the mainland, it was at the 1986 Great Dorset Steam Fair.

Six of these appliances with Merryweather 100-foot turntable ladders were built for the National Fire Service in 1942. They were based on the Leyland TD7 bus chassis and incorporated the half cab driving position from this design. The four-section ladder was driven from the vehicle engine and could be raised to 100 feet in thirty seconds. This example has been preserved in NFS grey livery and was at Rushmoor Arena in 1986. Similar GLW 419 later passed to the City of Lincoln Fire Service and is preserved by the Lincolnshire Vintage Vehicle Society in its later Lincoln red livery.

This 28-hp Bedford lorry was supplied to the RAF in 1942 as a military drinking water carrier. In 1945 it was sent to Alderney in the Channel Islands. In 1947 it was acquired by the States of Guernsey Airport, fitted with a Coventry Climax pump, and used as a fire tender. In 1972 it was transferred to Alderney Airport, where it worked until finally being withdrawn from service in 1977. It retained its Alderney registration number and appeared at Brighton on a number of occasions in the 1980s.

BUX 28 is an Albion SPKE127 with John Kerr bodywork in Braidwood style. It was ordered by Wellington Rural District Council but was delivered to the National Fire Service in 1941. It was transferred to Bridgnorth and then sold by Shropshire Fire Brigade to Robert Owen for their Kings Hill factory at Darleston. It was with the now defunct West Midlands Fire Engine Preservation Group. This was photographed leaving the Sandwell Rally at West Bromwich in 1984.

This 1943 Austin K4 Escape Carrier fire appliance was built to the Home Office specification for NFS vehicles and fitted with a Bayley ladder. It was allocated to the Pembrokeshire Fire Service for use at Pembroke Dock where it remained, latterly as a reserve vehicle at Milford Haven until 1973. It then stood in the open, outside a small museum for ten years until passing to an owner in Hampshire in 1983. Restoration was completed in 1986 and it was entered in the rally at Rushmoor Arena near Aldershot in July of that year.

This 1943 Dodge was supplied to the NFS as a mobile dam unit for use where water mains had been damaged by bombing. It passed to a private brigade after the war where it remained until the late 1970s. It was found in a derelict state in 1983 and since renovated. This was it at Rushmoor Arena in 1985.

Not all the NFS vehicles were designed to fight fires! GXH 355 was a 1943 Austin K2 mobile canteen. It served with No. 2 Fire Service in London during the war and later with Glamorgan Fire Service until 1975.

GXN 219 is one of a batch of fifty Austin K4s built for the NFS with Merryweather turntable ladders in 1943. This was taken in the period setting of the Crich Tramway Village.

Also lettered for the NFS, but in red livery, is GXN 205. Great Dorset Steam Fair, 2022.

A rare demonstration of fire fighting with a preserved fire engine. This event took place at the open day held at the Science Museum reserve collection at Wroughton airfield near Swindon in September 1988. The vehicle is GXN 231, another former NFS Austin K4 with Merryweather turntable ladder. Three working examples of these vehicles survive.

Fire-fighting Vehicles in Preservation

This 1944 Bedford QL four-wheel-drive vehicle GYR 786 worked at Morecambe Bay Fire Station. It was then kept at the Fylde Country Life Museum until purchased by the present owner in 2014. This was at the Great Dorset Steam Fair in 2019.

KRH 806 is one of ten similar turntable fire escapes built by Merryweather for the NFS and dates from 1949. This engine served at Hull. Based on an AEC chassis, the bonnet and radiator were built by Merryweather and only the design of the wheel hubs gives a clue to the AEC chassis. This was taken at Battersea Park on 2 May 1987 prior to taking part in the Run to Brighton the following day. This is now preserved in North Wales.

Seen arriving at Brighton in 2014, JUE 612 is a 1949 Dennis F2, one of the last open-cab fire appliances built. It was supplied as a works fire engine for British Thompson Houston at their Rugby works. It was lettered for Surrey Fire Brigade on this occasion having been used for film work. This vehicle was later nearly lost when the trailer carrying it back from a restoration in the Midlands caught fire on a motorway. Fortunately, the vehicle was saved and after another restoration job it was back at Brighton in 2022.

Also dating from 1949, this Land Rover Series 1 was bought by Tweedale & Smalley for their Globe Works at Castleton, near Rochdale. It was converted to a fire tender working with a 1939 Gwynne fire pump trailer. It was restored from 2006 using an original photograph obtained from the Manchester Fire Museum. Brighton, 2019.

British Vehicles of the 1950s

Probably the most unusual vehicle in this book, this *c.* 1950s Lister three-wheel truck was used at the Lister Petter factory in Dursley, Gloucestershire, where these trucks were made. Presumably accessibility within the confined spaces of the plant was more important than speed. Seen at the Gloucestershire Steam & Vintage Extravaganza in 2016.

This pump escape fire engine was built on an AEC Regent III bus chassis in 1950 and worked at Douglas with the Isle of Man Fire Service. In 1972 it came to the UK and the IOM registration NMN 50 was changed to EDM 893J. It has changed hands several times since then, the present owner purchasing it in 2007. Since 2014 a more suitable age-related number YXG 872 has been carried, as seen here at Brooklands in 2016.

OMA 353 is a 1951 Dennis F1 with a late example of a Braidwood body. This was supplied to ICI Ltd at their Runcorn Works. It was on display at the Crich Tramway Museum by the Derby Fire Engine Society on a visit in 1984. The F1 model was mostly for export so there are very few examples in these islands. There is one example in Ireland.

This 1951 Morris Commercial LC has a body built by Fisher Ludlow for their own works fire brigade. It was in use until 1980.

The Austin K4 continued to be built into the 1950s but this 1952 example has the later enclosed radiator. A number of these were purchased by Cornwall County Fire Brigade to replace wartime vehicles and were based at the smaller fire stations. NRL 361 was at Battersea Park in May 1984, before the London–Brighton Run the following day.

This Bedford was supplied to the City of Birmingham in 1952. The bodywork is by Wilsdon but Prestage may have been involved in the conversion of the SB bus chassis for fire engine use. It has a 4.9-litre petrol engine. This is now kept at the Wythall Bus Museum where it was on display in 1999.

The bonneted Leyland Comet chassis was built principally as a truck, although some were used as the basis for coach bodies. Surrey Fire Brigade bought five with petrol engines in 1951–52. Bodywork was by Windover of Hendon, who also bodied coaches at this time. In 1965, boundary changes saw four of the Comets including this one pass to the London Fire Brigade. At least two of the Comets survive and RPG 22, which worked at Sutton until 1966, visited Brighton in 1987.

Fire-fighting vehicles come in all sizes! This 1952 Morris Minor was specially constructed for use in confined spaces between vehicle assembly lines at the Morris Cowley plant. When entered at Brighton in 1985 it was still in use, principally as a foam carrier.

Dating from 1953 and registered in Edinburgh, this AEC/Merryweather turntable escape was in the fleet of the Lowland & Borders Fire Brigade. This was sent to Merryweather to have a mechanical ladder converted to hydraulic and was re-cabbed too. The ladder is 105 feet rather than the traditional 100 feet. This was taken a long way from its former operating area, at the Ardingly Showground, Sussex, in July 1984.

A 1953 Commer Superpoise with a dated open-cab New World-style body, JBD 819 was a works fire engine for the British Timken bearing works in Northampton. The bodywork was by Mulliner of Northampton, a coachbuilding company dating back to 1760. When seen at Peterborough in 1985 it was lettered as Duston Coachworks Ltd, who were a car repair and coachworks company in Northampton and who restored it.

Seen in the grounds of Clare Castle, Suffolk, with the castle ruins in the background, ORT 875 is 1953 Commer QX water tender that entered service with the Suffolk & Ipswich Fire Service. It served at Clare until 1976 and then with a factory at Haverhill. The present owners acquired it in 1996. This was bodied by Cuerden of Blackburn, who bodied only a handful of fire engines.

RUM 966 is a 1953 Dennis F8 fire engine, one of five built for Leeds City Fire Brigade. It is powered by a Rolls-Royce petrol engine. Although the crew compartment behind the driver is enclosed there are no side doors as entry is from the rear, like the earlier 'New World' appliances. Leeds was one of very few brigades to order 'New World' bodies after the Second World War. Taken at Dartford in 2009.

Fire-fighting Vehicles in Preservation

A regular at Brighton and other events throughout the south-east, I AMX is a 1954 Dennis F12 which was new to the Middlesex Fire Brigade at Staines. When the county of Middlesex was abolished in the 1965 local government reforms it passed to Surrey until withdrawn in 1973. In 1991 it was bought by six firemen from Leatherhead, who have restored and maintained it since. This is fitted with a Rolls-Royce B80 straight eight petrol engine.

The Essex County Fire & Rescue Service were out in force at Brighton in 2007 with five vehicles that served the county entered from the Essex Fire Museum, which opened at Grays that year. On the left is WTW 749, a 1953 Dennis F12 pump/escape which served at Grays from new until 1969. In the middle HNO 247B is a 1964 AEC/Merryweather turntable fire escape which was based at Basildon for twenty-five years. On the right is OWC 629, a 1962 Dennis F28 which served at Maldon.

OXT 779 was supplied to the London Fire Brigade in 1954 as an emergency tender at Lambeth Fire Station. It carried crew and equipment to support larger or more specialised call outs. This was based on an AEC Regent III bus chassis with Merryweather bodywork. Note the LFB badge on the radiator rather than the normal AEC badge.

There are a pair of these 1954 Morris Commercial fire engines that survive – GRX 41 and GRX 42. They were supplied to Berkshire Fire Brigade and have bodywork by Wadham Stringer – a company that would later be associated with bodying buses and coaches in the 1980s–90s. These were designated as hose reel tenders.

This is the only fire engine I have seen with this style of Leyland cab, which were usually found on lorries of this period. NWR 249 was built for the West Riding Fire Service in 1954 by John Morris & Son of Salford on a Leyland Beaver chassis and was one of only two such vehicles built. It has a Magirus 100-foot four-section steel turntable ladder and 500-gpm Coventry Climax pump taken from a 1939 trailer pump. It served at Batley, then Keighley, and then passed to the Yorkshire Fire Museum in 1974.

Land Rovers continued to find employment both with fire brigades and as works fire appliances where their smaller size could be an advantage. This 1955 series 1 was used by EMI at their Hayes factory for many years. It was bought for preservation in 1986 and entered at Brighton the following year. This has been reregistered.

PLF 623 is one of thirteen 1956 Fordson Thames 500E Firefly appliances that were ordered by the Ministry of Supply and used mostly at Royal Ordnance factories. This one was at ROF Glascoed. Fitted with bodies by Wadham Brothers of Waterlooville, they were built on a 3-ton chassis, and fitted with a diminutive 'cost-cutter' four-cylinder OHV petrol engine of 3,611cc and were perhaps somewhat ambitiously designated as pump foam tenders (P/FoT). They only carried 150 gallons of water and 36 gallons of foam compound in a separate tank, along with a Coventry Climax major pump. This was at a the 1984 'Wheels of Yesterday' rally in Battersea Park that followed the London–Brighton Run.

A pair of the famous mid-1950s 'Green Goddess' Bedfords. These had a 4.9-litre six-cylinder petrol engine which also drove a Sigmund 900-gpm pump. They carry registrations in series that were partly reserved for Government owned vehicles. These two were seen at a rally in St Albans in 2011.

RXP 763 is another 'Green Goddess' Bedford dating from 1956. This was originally used by the Colchester Fire Brigade. When rallied at Brighton in 2016 it had just 2,000 miles on the clock.

RYX 491 is another AFS Bedford but this is bodied as a command unit. Seen at Billericay, Essex, in 2011.

Yet another Bedford, 373 ALC was based on the standard Army Recovery Vehicle. This was fitted with a 3-ton maximum capacity swinging jib and a 7-ton main winch. 373 ALC was originally supplied to Devon but ended up with Cornwall County Fire Brigade as seen here at the Redhill Rally in 2005.

RYX 26 is a 1954 Commer Q4. It was built as a tipper/winch and converted as a so-called 'Bikini' unit in 1955. These were part of the Auxiliary Fire Services mobile columns to be used in event of nuclear war or other emergencies. They carried inflatable rafts and portable pumps. When the AFS was disbanded in 1968 the vehicles were stored for another thirty years. This example is seen with its full equipment now restored, having been purchased without it. Basingstoke, 1998.

Registered at Inverness in 1955, JST 314 is a Bedford with HCB body that worked for the Northern Fire Brigade. Now a long way from its former base, this was at a rally at Netley, Hampshire, in 1986. This had no built-in pump but towed a trailer pump and was designated 'hose reel tender'.

JTY 552 is a 1955 Dennis F8 new to Northumberland Fire Brigade. It was one of only twenty-six Miles-bodied F8s built. It had no built-in pump, just a light portable pump that makes it a water tender type A, not the more typical type B.

YKP 177 was supplied to the Kent Fire Brigade in 1956. This used an AEC Regent III bus chassis and was fitted with a mechanical Merryweather ladder dating from 1938. The engine was stationed at Folkestone.

The Dennis F101 of 1956 was a breakthrough as being the first Dennis fire appliance to be powered by a diesel engine. Only thirty-eight of this model were made, all for the London Fire Brigade. SLW 178 was sold in 1979 after five years at the training centre. Taken at Battersea Park in 1986.

This Bedford with Miles bodywork dating from *c.* 1957 was supplied to the Brecon & Radnor Joint Fire Brigade. This was taken at Carrog on the Llangollen Railway in 2001. The polished, unpainted aluminium side panels were fashionable in the 1950s/60s, although normally the front of the engine would be red.

Another Bedford/Miles vehicle but this has been rebuilt as a towing lorry at some stage in its working life The original owning fire brigade was Herefordshire but the vehicle has been reregistered in preservation. Seen at Ardingly in 1989.

WBJ 90 is a 1957 Bedford A4L chassis with Carmichael body sold to the Suffolk & Ipswich Fire Service. It saw use at Hadleigh before being sold on to Westgate Brewery in 1977. The appliance carries 400 gallons of water, has a 500-gallon-per-minute pump, a 35-foot ladder and carried a crew of six.

Ransomes, formerly known as Ransomes, Sims & Jefferies Ltd, are a major engineering company from Ipswich dating back to 1869, who manufactured a range of agricultural equipment, traction engines, lawn mowers, etc. WVF 123 is a 1957 Land Rover which was acquired as a works fire engine. This was seen in Ipswich at the start of the 2022 Ipswich–Felixstowe Road Run.

Fire-fighting Vehicles in Preservation

Another works fire engine, this 1957 Morris was used by the MG Works Fire Brigade.

When this AEC Mercury turntable ladder was supplied to the London Fire Brigade in 1958, it was the first turntable ladder in the brigade to have an enclosed cab. It was also their only AEC Mercury to have a mechanical rather than hydraulic ladder, the ladder being a Magirus example which was removed from a 1932 Dennis appliance. This was at Battersea Park on 3 May 1986, prior to taking part in the Run to Brighton on the following day. Note the chimneys of Battersea Power Station against the skyline.

79 GPK is the sole survivor of three Austin FE foam/salvage tenders bought by Surrey Fire Brigade in 1958. They had a small pump to empty flooded basements and carried a large quantity of foam to assist other machines at oil fires. 79 GPK was originally based at Epsom and remained in service until 1974. The bodies were built in the brigade's own workshops at Reigate. Brighton, 1992.

XBJ 941 is a Bedford S type water tender with Carmichael bodywork new to the Suffolk & Ipswich Fire Service in 1958. It served at four different locations before being sold to the US Air Force and based at RAF Woodbridge. The body is constructed from steel and alloy bodywork, a similar build process that was adopted by Alfred Miles. This was to a higher specification than the normal method of ash framing incorporating marine ply. It has been in private ownership since 1995.

This Bedford TL turntable ladder was new to Kent Fire Brigade in 1959. It was stationed at Margate until 1972, then at Westwood until 1982. It has a Magirus ladder fitted by John Morris of Salford. Now owned by D. W. Davis Ltd, it was at the Chiltern Steam Rally in 1995.

When this Dennis F8 fire engine was delivered to the Wokingham Fire Station of Berkshire Fire Brigade in 1959 it had an open cab so as not to foul the low-arched doorway. When the fire station was later moved to a new location, UBL 465 was sent back to Dennis Bros to have a new cab fitted. Knowl Hill, 1999.

UBL 464 is a 1959 Karrier Gamecock with Carmichael bodywork which was new to the Berkshire & Reading Fire Brigade. It was transferred to Oxfordshire Fire Service in 1974 as a result of boundary changes. Seen at Basingstoke in 2013.

The Austin Gypsy was Austin's answer to the Land Rover. 82 ERL is a 1959 model, one of a number bought by Cornwall County Fire Brigade. This later served at Falmouth dockyard until the mid-1980s. It is fitted with a front-mounted Coventry Climax pump. It is seen alongside a 1964 Land Rover at the 2003 Great Dorset Steam Fair.

British Vehicles of the 1960s

RJD 344 was new in 1960 to the West Ham Fire Brigade, London. It is an AEC Mercury with Merryweather foam tender bodywork. Under the local government reforms of 1965, the County Borough of West Ham was merged with neighbour East Ham to become the London Borough of Newham. The two borough's fire brigades were absorbed into the London Fire Brigade. RJD 344 was withdrawn in 1978 but passed into preservation as seen here in LFB colours at Netley in 1989. This was subsequently rebuilt as a lorry (see p. 95).

This 1960 Bedford RL was an airport fire tender at Oxford for all its working life until retired in 1978, after which it saw occasional use as a snowplough. The bodywork is by Fire Armour. Brighton, 2002.

3991 PX is one of a batch of 1960 Land Rover Series 2 purchased by West Sussex Fire Brigade from Masons at Chichester in mid-1961. When purchased they were supplied in Ferguson grey with county cream wheels. The brigade workshops converted them into hose reel tenders fitting a 70-gallon tank, one first-aid hose reel and also a light portable pump. It was at Midhurst throughout its life and was presented at Brighton in 2016 in the 'Coventry Yellow' livery.

4589 PX is a 1960 Bedford J5 pump/escape with bodywork by HCB of Totton. It served with West Sussex Fire Brigade at Steyning and later Storrington. Withdrawn after eighteen years, it was auctioned and saw several other owners before being retrieved from a scrapyard for preservation.

97 SPK dates from 1960 and was one of twenty Dennis F24 fire engines delivered to Surrey Fire Brigade between 1958 and 1961. This was new to Esher Fire Station. Retired in 1978, it then passed to the Bluebell Railway until 1983. It has been in preservation with the present owner since 1985 and has appeared in films and used for fundraising. In 1990 it was called out again to assist in tackling heathland fires on Horsell and Chobham Commons. Seen here at Brighton in 1994.

Also with Surrey Fire Brigade, 221 VPB is a 1961 Dennis F27 with a Magirus DL30H 100-foot turntable ladder. It cost approximately £12,000 when new and was in use, mainly at Chertsey, until 1978. It then stood in the open for the next thirty years before restoration beckoned. It completed the Brighton Run in 2013.

Taken at Woodcote in 2011, LEU 250 is a 1961 Bedford J2 fire engine with HCB body new to the Brecon & Radnor Joint Fire Brigade. It served at Abercrave and then Llandridnod Wells until retired in 1978. The 133-bhp petrol engine does approximately 6 miles per gallon.

MFO 813 is a 1962 AEC Mercury with Carmichael body new to Reading Fire Service, originally registered 3 BBL. After withdrawal it was sold to a travelling showman from Colchester who removed the water tank and pumps and fitted a generator. Woodcote, 2009.

As well as the conventional Land Rover jeep, the company made a forward control version. REG 999 is a 1962 model that was used by the Peterborough Volunteer Fire Brigade and has Dennis bodywork. This was seen in 2022 at Christchurch Park, Ipswich, setting off for the Ipswich–Felixstowe Road Run.

A 1962 or 1963 Bedford TK turntable fire escape that was delivered to Luton, then passed to Bedfordshire Fire Brigade in 1974. It was later with Westgate brewery at Bury St Edmunds. This was seen at North Weald in 1989. Note the screw jacks either side of the rear wheels to give stability when the ladder is deployed.

CBY 1 was delivered to Croydon Fire Brigade in 1963. Croydon was one of three County Borough Councils in the Greater London area that, like East Ham and West Ham, had their own fire brigades. When London local government was reformed in 1965 these three brigades, along with Middlesex, all passed to an enlarged London Fire Brigade. This AEC Mercury/Merryweather remained in use until 1984 and was then retained as a heritage vehicle for special duties.

Dennis F107 type 314 FLM was built as a recovery vehicle for the London Fire Brigade in 1963 using the shortened chassis of a turntable ladder prototype and fitted with a Herbert Morris crane. It was based at Clapham Fire Station for most of its operational life. It was sold in 1977 and later worked as a recovery vehicle for Wincanton Transport before being bought for preservation in the 1990s. Amberley Museum, 1995.

CYY 352C is a 1965 Austin Gypsy supplied to the Auxiliary Fire Service. It would have been used as a crew carrier to form part of a mobile fire column. Now preserved in Hampshire and seen at Basingstoke in 2011.

BFE 516C is a Carmichael conversion from a 1965 Series IIA forward control Land Rover that was a works engine for the Ruston Bucyrus excavator works at Lincoln. Woodcote Rally, 2008.

This Bedford was built in 1965 for the AFS. It passed to Clwyd Fire Service in 1988 as a foam carrier. It carried two large foam containers and 25-litre drums of Hi Ex. It also carried inductors and Hi Ex fans, etc. It had a Ratcliff tail lift to help access (since removed). Since this photo was taken in 2004 it has been repainted in AFS green.

Registered at Luton, this 1965 Bedford TK water tender was new to Bedfordshire Fire Brigade and stationed at Potten. It could carry 400 gallons of water and could pump at 600 gallons per minute. Now owned by D. W. Davis Ltd, Great Missenden, it is a regular at the nearby Chiltern Steam Rally at Prestwood where it was taken in 1993.

Fire-fighting Vehicles in Preservation

In 1964 the Chief Fire Officer of Kent Fire Brigade invited all ranks to submit ideas for a new fleet of fire appliances. The first engine incorporating the best of these suggestions entered service at Dartford in 1966, followed by a further forty-eight over the next four years. Typical of these is this 1966 Commer K2 water tender with a HCB body, which worked out of Cranbrook Fire Station. This was at Battersea Park in 1985.

The Bedford TK chassis was used as the basis for many fire engines. This 1967 model for Hampshire Fire Service was bodied in their own workshops, one of the very few brigade workshops to build pumping appliances from scratch. It served at Romsey until 1982 when it became a spare at Winchester. It was then sold to Lancing Bagnall as a works appliance until bought for preservation in 1994. Taken at Netley Marsh Steam & Craft Show in 2006.

MLV 606F is a 1968 AEC/Merryweather supplied to the Merseyside Fide Brigade and has a 100-foot turntable ladder. This is one of the few examples built with the 'Ergonomic'-style cab introduced in 1965 and is powered by an AEC AV505 diesel engine.

A particular specialised form of fire-fighting vehicle was developed for airfield use. One of the leading suppliers of such vehicles was the specialist maker Thornycroft, from Basingstoke. There is a Thornycroft Society keeping their legacy alive and vehicles from their collection can usually be seen at the Basingstoke Rally. KFF 132 is one of the vehicles owned by the society and was seen in 1998. This is a former military dual-purpose Mark1/1A bodied by Foamite. This is not the original registration but an 'age-related' one issued by the DVLA in the 1990s.

British Vehicles of the 1970s

Dating from *c.* 1970 this Dennis F108 rescue tender from the London Fire Brigade was preserved and is seen participating in the 2011 Lord Mayor's Show.

Another example of an AEC with the 'Ergonomic' cab design. FWE 984J was supplied to the City of Sheffield Fire Brigade in 1970 with Merryweather bodywork. It was used until 1981 and was then at the training school in Rotherham until withdrawn and sold in 1983. It has a 400-gallon water tank, 1,000-gpm pump and 50-foot wheeled escape. Rushmoor Arena, 1990.

Not all fire engines were red! This 1970 Dennis D series was delivered new to West Sussex Fire Brigade at Littlehampton in 'Coventry Yellow', as seen here. In 1980 it was relegated to driver training and repainted red. Withdrawn in 1988 and now restored to original condition, this was on display at the Dennis Works Open Day at Guildford in May 2019. It is fitted with a 4.2-litre Jaguar engine.

Another 1970 Dennis in a different colour scheme. DWT 472H was an F46 model with the West Riding service. Seen at the trolleybus museum at Sandtoft in 1988. A small number of brigades went white in the 1970s. The colour scheme did not generally last long, Grampian being an exception.

At Basingstoke in 1995 was this 1970 Thornycroft Nubian airfield fire appliance with Carmichael body, which was used at Bristol Airport. Note the roof-mounted foam-spraying apparatus.

This 1972 Leyland Mastiff water tanker with tank/body by Ferguson was new to Hampshire Fire Brigade and initially stationed at Basingstoke. It later saw use at Fordingbridge. It was out of service in 1988. Only a few Mastiffs ever became fire appliances. Seen at Basingstoke, 2015.

These two Dennis appliances formerly with Essex Fire Brigade were entered on the 2008 London–Brighton Run. POO 464K on the right dates from 1971 and is a pump which was based on Canvey Island until 1986, while AVW 980L on the left is from 1973. This was one of a pair of foam tender/escape appliances and was stationed at Basildon to deal with the various petrochemical sites along the Thames. It passed to the Shell Haven oil refinery in 1989 and then via two other owners before being sold into preservation. AVW 980L has a Simonitor, one of only about a dozen built by Simon Engineering. They extended to 15 metres and were a precursor of today's telesquirts.

This 1977 Dennis D series served with the Devon Fire Brigade and was stationed at Braunton. Devon had slamshut lockers quite late after other brigades chose roller shutters. Seen at Newark in 2017.

OYT 517R is a *c.* 1977 fire control unit that served with London Fire Brigade. This is based on a Ford R1014 bus/coach chassis with a Willowbrook bus body shell fitted out by Anglo Coachbuilders. Alongside is ACG 797C, a 1965 Bedford fire engine, ex-Hampshire Fire Brigade. These were on display at the open day held at the Science Museum reserve collection at Wroughton Airfield near Swindon on 11 September 1988.

British Vehicles of the 1980s and 1990s

An unusual vehicle entered at Brighton in 2005, EBB 847W is a 1980 Shelvoke & Drewry type WY. S&D became a major supplier of fire appliances from 1980s, having previously been more typically associated with the manufacture of dustcarts and gully emptiers. It was bought by the Tyne & Wear Metropolitan Fire Brigade and originally had a foam tender body by Chubb Fire with two tanks carrying a total of 800 gallons of foam. In the 1990s the brigade moved away from dedicated foam tenders and the vehicle was converted to its present form. It has a Perkins V8 640 engine, which was developed specifically for use in fire appliances.

Dennis continued as a major manufacturer of fire appliances into the 1980s and 1990s. Two typical vehicles from this period are seen together at the Basingstoke rally in 2016. ANO 167X is a 1981 RS133 model from Essex Fire Brigade which served at Colchester, while D617 NDV is a 1986 RS131 model from Devon bodied by Saxon Sanbec.

P74 HHP is a 1996 Dennis Sabre with John Dennis (JDC) body purchased by Warwickshire Fire Brigade as a rescue pump ladder engine. It later passed to Kent International Airport at Manston. It was purchased for preservation in 2016 and entered at Brighton in 2019, qualifying under the twenty-one years minimum age rule.

European Vehicles

Dating from 1921, this Magirus fire escape was on the premises of dealers Preston Services, Preston, Kent, at their rally in 2009.

This is a 1927 Ahrens-Fox fire appliance from Holland which was entered on the London–Brighton Run in 2009–11. Little information was supplied other than that it had one owner from new and was entered by ROTEB, Rotterdam.

From 1991 to 1995 the HCVS London–Brighton Run was sponsored by Scania. This led to several interesting vehicles being brought over from Sweden each year to participate. In 1994 this 1928 Chevrolet was entered. It had been imported to Sweden as a lorry but was converted locally in 1934 with a Swedish-built Albin Motors pump. Note the white uniforms and silver-coloured helmets of the crew – a contrast to British practice.

This 1933 Mercedes-Benz LF16 pump from West Germany was entered in the 1989 and 1991 London–Brighton Runs. Entered by Mercedes-Benz, it was the property of the Daimler-Benz Museum, who purchased it in 1978 from the Stuttgart Fire Brigade.

In 1993 this 1933 Volvo pump was another vehicle brought over from Sweden under the Scania sponsorship. It served at Ljungby Fire Station from 1973 to 1971, after which it was preserved.

Although the Scania sponsorship ended in 1995, some vehicles have continued to come from Sweden for the London–Brighton Run. In 2008 this 1931 Scania-Vabis pump/escape was entered. This has been restored and maintained by employees and former employees of Stockholm Fire Brigade.

Entered from Germany in 1993 was this 1949 fire appliance built by Metz on an Opel Blitz 2500cc, 50-hp chassis. It was purchased from Richenbach in the Black Forest in 1990.

A later Opel Blitz from 1959. This also has a Metz body and pump and was used at Eichenau, Bavaria, and later at a factory in Sonthofen. It was bought out of service in 1990. This was entered on the London–Brighton Run in 1991 and was photographed at Crystal Palace Park the evening beforehand.

This 1959 American-built Willys fire tender was an entrant at Brighton in 2005. This had travelled from Skien in Norway.

This Ford Taunos van from Germany was seen at a rally on Canvey Island in 2017. As it has been given a year-specific British registration, KBY 399C, this would indicate that it dates from 1965. It was used by the fire department at Stadt Bad Munstereifel.

This 1967 Scania-Vabis 76 fire appliance from Sweden was brought to Brighton in 2008 to accompany the 1931 Scania-Vabis (see p. 83).

This Magirus fire tender, probably from Germany, was at entrant at a rally in Lingfield, Surrey, in 1999.

Representing French practice, this Berliet turntable fire escape was taken at a rally in Sussex in 1996. Berliet vehicles were made from 1899 onwards. The company became part of Citroen in 1967 and then was acquired by Renault in 1974. The name was phased out by 1980.

The legendary Citroen H series van was made from 1947 to 1981, with nearly half a million built. Many can still be found serving as static food outlets. This example, seen at the same rally but in 1997, served as a fire tender in France.

American Vehicles

This 1919 American La France 75 fire pumper was supplied to Kirkwood City Fire Department, Missouri, and later sold on to the Huron Fire Department, South Dakota. It is fitted with a massive 14.5-litre six-cylinder petrol engine and is capable of speeds up to 70 mph. The pump could deliver water at 750 gallons per minute. This was imported in 2001 and acquired by the present owners in 2015, who entered it at Brighton in 2016. The bodywork, wooden spoke wheels and paintwork are largely original.

Also dating from 1919 is this Model T Ford, which was shipped over to Britain in 1990 from Detroit, Michigan. This was entered at Brighton in 2002 and 2004. It is seen alongside 1925 Austin ML 255 (see p. 18).

Fire-fighting Vehicles in Preservation

At Brighton in 2013 we see this 1927 American La France Fire Engine. It was made at Elmira, New York State, and spent most of its working life at Eminence, New York State. This is fitted with a six-cylinder 14.7-litre petrol engine.

This 1930 Mack BB was purchased in Kansas in 2004 and imported in 2009. It completed the London–Brighton Run in 2011, although at the time bodywork restoration was not complete. In 2015 this had been completed and the engine was judged Best in Class. It was originally employed at Guthrie, Oklahoma.

An early example of an American articulated ladder escape, this American La France was at a rally in Redhill in 1990.

This 1938 Mack tractor unit was new to Baltimore Fire Department where it was coupled with this Hayes Ariel ladder that dates from 1889 and was originally horse-drawn. The Mack served until 1962, then was held in reserve until 1974 when sold to Dry Gulch Fire Department, Fort Lauderdale. This was taken at the 1986 Knowl Hill Rally.

This is a 1942 GMC CCKW 353 type fire tender. After the Second World War many military vehicles were sold to Europe to help rebuild countries. This one went to Morlaix Fire Station in Brittany, France, where it remained in use until 1993. Brighton, 2005.

Also at the Knowl Hill Rally in 1986 was this 1950 Ward La France pump engine, which spent its working life with Archville Fire Department, New York. It has a 750-gallons-per-minute pump and is capable of 70 mph but at only 4 miles per gallon. It was imported in 1986.

At Knowl Hill in 1988, this 1956 GMC 630 worked for Morehead City Fire Department, North Carolina. It had been imported to the UK in 1987. Note the winged creature motif on top of the bonnet – not your usual fire engine fitting!

This 1958 Mack was with the fire brigade at the City of Hamilton, the capital of Bermuda, where it ran until 1992. This is fitted with a Waterous pump delivering 1,250 gallons per minute. Brighton, 1993.

Arriving at Brighton in 1993 was this 1959 American La France 9005 series which served at Ephrata, Pennsylvania, until 1992 when it was shipped to England. This was originally fitted with V12 petrol engine but this was changed in 1988 to a Caterpillar V8 diesel. There would be plenty of warning of its approach as it has a bell and siren at either ends of the front bumper and two horns on the cab roof.

This 1960 Mack C95 was supplied to Woodbury Fire Department, New Jersey, and ran for them until 1989. It was imported in 1990 and entered at Brighton in 1991.

As with the 1938 Mack articulated unit seen earlier, this 1969 Oren Roanoak tractor unit is paired with an earlier ladder, built in 1949. This was at Richmond, Virginia, Bureau of Fire, Pennsylvania, until 1991 when it was imported to the UK. It was then entered in the 1992 London–Brighton Run. At first it was allocated UK registration Q807 RGF but when seen at Lingfield in 1999 it had been given an age-related registration BGC 383G.

With an age related 'H' suffix registration this articulated unit dates from 1970. This was at the rally in Redhill in 2005. Fitted with a Hahn/Grove 100-foot aerial ladder, this served the City of Bethesda, Maryland.

This is a 1988 Ford fire appliance powered by a Caterpillar 250-hp engine, which served at Flemington, New Jersey. In 2001 it attended the 9/11 tragedy in New York. After being retired in 2008 it was brought to England. Seen at the Basingstoke Festival of Transport in 2013, it has also been entered on the London–Brighton Run on two occasions.

This turntable escape was used at Catawissa, Pennsylvania. This has a hydraulic platform ladder, as well as some shorter conventional ladders. It was at Crystal Palace Park in 1994 the day before the London–Brighton Run but was not listed as an entrant in the Run.

Rebuilt Former Fire-fighting Vehicles

This vehicle with its machinery carrier beaver tail body may not look much like a fire engine, but the design of the crew cab gives a clue to its origins. 209 HAT is a 1964 AEC Mercury MkII new to Hull Fire Brigade. It was bought by a Mr Hatcher from Swindon in 1989 as a derelict chassis/cab and rebuilt as seen to carry a 1947 Fordson Major E27N tractor. This was photographed in Bath on 7 September 1997 nearing the end of the HCVS Bournemouth–Bath Road Run. Although 209 HAT is a Hull registration from 1964, this may be a personalised reregistration as there is no record of a Hull appliance with this number.

The origins of this AEC lorry are not obvious as it has not only been rebodied but reregistered. However, HHF 84 started life as County Borough of West Ham RJD 344 (see p. 65). It was photographed in this form at the Netley Marsh Steam & Craft Show near Southampton in July 1993. By 2000 it had been rebuilt again as a dropside lorry. Note the pivoted cab doors. This may have been made at the former Maudsley works at Alcester after they had been taken over by AEC.

Acknowledgements and Further Reading

Much of the information for this book has come from the excellent rally programmes produced for the HCVS London–Brighton Run. Other information has come from the rally programmes of other events, while details of the steam vehicles is provided in the Traction Engine Register. Unfortunately, there is no published list of all known preserved fire engines (or other commercial lorries) at present.

Special thanks to Peter Williams for information supplied about vehicles and for checking the text.

Baker, Eddie, *Fire Engines* (Shire, 2018)
Bonner, Robert F., *Fire Engines of North West England* (Nostalgia Road, 2003)
Fisher, Aidan, *HCB-Angus: A Pictorial Record* (Amberley Publishing, 2013)
Henry, Andrew, Henderson, Ronald, and Toomey, John, *Classic Post-war British Fire Engines: Fire Brigades in 1973* (Amberley Publishing, 2022)
Henderson, Ronald, *British Steam Fire Engines* (Amberley Publishing, 2016)
Hutchinson, Barry, *Dennis Fire Engines* (Amberley Publishing, 2015)
Johnson, Brian, *The Traction Engine Register, 13th edition* (Horsham, Southern Counties Historic Vehicles Preservation Trust, 2020)
Rowley, Simon, *Airport Crash Tenders* (Nostalgia Road, 2000)
Rowley, Simon, *Fire Engines of the 1950s and 1960s* (Nostalgia Road, 1999)
Wallington, Neil, *The World Encyclopedia of Fire Engines* (Lorenz, 2022)
Williams, Peter, *West Ham & its Fire Brigade: An Illustrated History 1800–1965* (EB Books, 2019)

Websites:
Fire Service Preservation Group, https://fspg.org.uk
dennissociety.org.uk
www.fire-engine-photos.com